COYOTES

COYOTES

SANDRA LEE

THE CHILD'S WORLD

PHOTO CREDITS

W. Perry Conway: front cover, back cover,
2, 9, 13, 17, 18, 19, 21, 23, 24, 26-27, 31
Jeanne Drake: 10, 14, 28
Leonard Lee Rue III: 6

Printed in the United States of America.

Distributed to schools and libraries in the United States by
ENCYCLOPAEDIA BRITANNICA EDUCATIONAL CORP.
310 South Michigan Avenue
Chicago, Illinois 60604

Library of Congress Cataloging-in-Publication Data
Lee, Sandra.
Coyotes / by Sandra Lee.
p. cm.
Summary: Introduces the physical and behavioral
characteristics of coyotes.
ISBN 0-89565-843-7
1. Coyotes--Juvenile literature. [1. Coyotes.] I. Title.
QL737.C22L44 1992 91-41150
599.74'442--dc20 CIP
AC

Dedicated to Native Americans and other friends of the Coyote

If you are ever in the deserts of the southwestern United States, you might be awakened early one morning by a strange sound. You may have thought there was nothing in the darkness, but a sad, long howl will convince you that there is. Soon the many coyotes living in the area will join in the chorus echoing across the canyons.

Howling is one of the social things that a coyote does with others of a group, or *pack*. The howling begins with a short bark or yap and turns into a long yell. After a minute or two there is a pause, and then the chorus begins again. It is not known for certain, but coyotes may howl to let others know their territory.

It is probably not surprising that coyotes are members of the dog family. They are closely related to wolves, foxes, and jackals. The coyote is sometimes called a prairie wolf. With their slender legs and bushy tails, coyotes look a lot like domestic dogs. A full-grown coyote is about the same size as a small collie.

A coyote's face is very expressive. It can show fear, curiosity, and affection, just like a puppy dog's. A coyote has very good hearing. It moves its pointed ears in the direction of sounds that are interesting to it. It can hear the slightest sound—even a mouse under the snow.

Coyotes are intelligent and adaptable animals. They are found throughout the United States and Canada, from the mountains of Alaska to the deserts of Arizona. Some even live in canyons near the city of Los Angeles! Coyotes also live as far south as Central America.

Because coyotes live in so many different places, they must be able to survive in a wide variety of climates. Those that live in northern climates adjust to the cold by growing thicker fur. Their fur is dark to hide them in the forests and underbrush. Coyotes that live in the desert have lighter-colored fur that blends with the mountains and sand. Their fur varies in color from reddish brown to gray and black.

Coyotes make very good parents. They mate and stay together for years. Baby coyotes are born in the spring. The mother makes a *den*, which is a hole or tunnel dug under the ground. The newborns are kept in the den, where they are protected from enemies. The parents sleep outside, curled up beside a bush or a rock. If they sense danger, they move the pups to a new den.

Usually there are five to seven pups in a litter. The mother nurses the pups until they are old enough to eat solid food. As the pups grow older, they come out of the den to be fed. The mother always stands nearby and keeps a lookout for danger. The father brings home food for the pups. He eats something, maybe a rabbit, then comes home and spits it up in front of the pups. It doesn't sound very appetizing, but to the pups it is baby food—not much chewing is needed!

Young coyotes play with one another and with the adults, just like other puppies do. Their favorite games are tag, hide-and-seek, and nip-and-run! The adults teach the young coyotes how to howl. In the fall, the pups go off to raise families of their own. Some of the young females may stay with the parents and form a pack.

Coyotes eat a wide variety of things. Their main food seems to be rodents—mice, gophers, or prairie dogs. They also enjoy grasshoppers and other insects. Though coyotes prefer to be alone, they get together to hunt and feed. Sometimes coyotes will even hunt with badgers. The coyote uses its keen sense of smell to find a rodent burrowing beneath the ground. Then the badger digs it up with its powerful claws. The coyote and the badger then share the meal!

Sometimes a pack of coyotes will chase elk, deer, or antelope. Coyotes are very fast runners. They can run at speeds of up to 40 miles per hour. This is faster than the speed limit in most cities!

Despite their speed, coyotes are not big enough to kill healthy deer. The only large animals they can catch are usually sick or dying. They chase these animals in relays, with one coyote taking over after another gets tired. After eating, the coyotes gather for a long howl before going their separate ways.

Unfortunately, the coyote has some habits that make it unpopular among farmers. Coyotes sometimes raid fields of ripe watermelons. Though they take only a bite or two out of each melon, they can destroy an entire crop.

Many livestock and sheep ranchers also dislike coyotes. They often blame coyotes for killing their animals. Actually, coyotes help the ranchers. They kill rodents and rabbits, which eat the same foods as the livestock. If there are plenty of rodents, coyotes do not bother large farm animals.

Coyotes are sometimes attacked by large predators such as wolves or pumas. Humans, however, are their greatest enemies. There are some federal and state programs that try to control the coyote population. Game wardens try to eliminate only the individual coyote that is causing a problem. Still the coyote survives, finding new places to live. The next time you wake before dawn, listen! Perhaps you will hear the song of the coyote.

THE CHILD'S WORLD
NATUREBOOKS

Wildlife Library

Alligators
Arctic Foxes
Bald Eagles
Beavers
Birds
Black Widows
Camels
Cheetahs
Coyotes
Dogs
Dolphins
Elephants
Fish
Giraffes
Insects
Kangaroos
Lions
Mammals
Monarchs
Musk-oxen
Octopuses
Owls
Penguins
Polar Bears
Primates
Rattlesnakes
Reptiles
Rhinoceroses
Seals and Sea Lions
Sharks
Snakes
Spiders
Tigers
Walruses
Whales
Wildcats
Wolves
Zebras

Space Library

Earth
Mars
The Moon
The Sun

Adventure Library

Glacier National Park
The Grand Canyon
Yellowstone National Park
Yosemite